Barbara-Ann Gale is a retired baby boomer who pursued a career in the legal and business world and is now transitioning to a new career as an author. She draws upon her academic background in child and abnormal psychology, earning a degree from McGill University, combined with her general interest in preparing children for the new demands of the digital age by increasing their awareness of the technical aspects of the devices they so handily use. She grew up in Montreal, Quebec, and is now a longtime resident in Toronto, Ontario.

Fallon's Digi-Bet
New World Alphabet
for the Digital Age

Barbara-Ann Gale

AUSTIN MACAULEY PUBLISHERS™

LONDON • CAMBRIDGE • NEW YORK • SHARJAH

Ordering Information
Quantity sales: Special discounts are available on quantity purchases by corporations, associations, and others. For details, contact the publisher at the address below.

Publisher's Cataloging-in-Publication data
Gale, Barbara-Ann
Fallon's Digi-Bet

ISBN 9781645752042 (Paperback)
ISBN 9781645752059 (Hardback)
ISBN 9781645752066 (ePub e-book)

Library of Congress Control Number: 2020920224

www.austinmacauley.com/us

First Published (2021)
Austin Macauley Publishers LLC
40 Wall Street, 33rd Floor, Suite 3302
New York, NY 10005
USA

mail-usa@austinmacauley.com
+1 (646) 5125767

To Fallon, my four-year-old great-niece, and to the generation of children everywhere who are facing the challenges and opportunities of the digital age in this brave new world.

Special thanks to Fallon Nichols for inspiring me to write this book and to her parents, my niece Krishna and husband Quincy. Many thanks to elder sister Dona and husband Althomme Pierre, who always lend me their ears. Thanks to F. Douglas Gay who has been with me on this journey through thick and thin. Thank you to the team at Austin Macauley for bringing this book to life and for believing in me.

I am a child of the Digital Age.
This is what I have to say.
Lots of things have changed, you know.
This is how I learn to grow.

I AM A CHILD...

A is for Apple but not the ones you eat.

It means a favorite tech company we love because
it is so sweet.

B is for Browser, an essential tool for looking
up websites and documents too.

It's a software app that processes code, HTML,
into words and pictures that flow, and surfing
the internet clicking as you go.

C is for Cookies but not the ones mom bakes.

Cookies follow us around when we land on a
website's ground.

D is for Digital in the Information Age.

Means using 0s and 1s from the binary code, to
convert language and data into instructions to
tell the computer where information goes.

F=01100110; A=01100001; L=01101100; O=01
N=01101110

E is for Emails or electronic mail,

which is how we send instant messages electronically
from one computer to another, super quick
and easily.

F is for Firewall, your computer's best defense

against hackers and bad actors who want access
to your data to give it back at your expense.

G is for Google, the most favored search engine.

It ranks web pages by content and key words,
and linkages between them which are the
most referred.

H is for Hyperlinks found in your documents.

You know when you meet them, they are blue
and underlined. The cursor placed upon them
promptly turns into a hand. Jumps you through
pages at hyper speed, gets you to the finish line
on command.

I is for Icons you first see on your screen when
you open your computer or cell phone, whichever
it be.

They visually represent programs and files or
anything else that makes computing worthwhile.

HOME WORK
NATURE
STORIES
MOVIES

J is for Java, we don't mean coffee, but a computer
language, or code, for the web that is
considered lofty.

When you search for information you input into your
browser, JavaScript converts it so the computer
understands, and then instantaneously executes
your plan.

K is for Keywords that help describe the content
and act as assistants to find out what you meant.

Search engines use them to create an index of
documents instantly found, or non-existent.

L for Linux, a system software for computers.

You can obtain it for free, unlike macOS and
Windows, where you must pay a fee.

M is for Machine Learning based on AI.

Artificial Intelligence that could make humans
irrelevant but at the same time makes robotics
heaven-sent.

TH LESSON
x 1 = 9
9 x 2 = 18
9 x 3 = 27
9 x 4 = 36

N is for Navigation of the web, of course, not water.

We surf the web looking for people, places, and encyclopedic info. Also, for streaming entertainment, viral and how-to videos. We navigate the information resources of website schemes and web designs, with template cascades to our find.

O is for Operating System, software your computer must have for it to come alive and perform essential functions on which we all rely.

OS is the platform on which other software programs run. The basic user interface that provides us so much fun.

P is for Protocol for transmitting data.

Refers to the rules computers must follow to exchange information and interact with each other, and to avoid the confusion of crosstalk and chatter.

Q is for queries or questions you have when you use your search engine with keywords in hand.

The computer retrieves the info you need by producing an index of results you then read.

SEARCH
the meaning of education?

R is for Random Access Memory or RAM, not
sheep that will roam without a software program.

Computers require memory or RAM so the
software they host can run as smooth as sand.

S is for Server, not the people who serve food.

We mean a computer that serves up data to
other computers on a network, making it a
breeze to finish our homework.

SERVER

T is for Toolbar, a set of icons or buttons, not the kind you find on your shirt and pant bottoms.

A toolbar forms part of a software program's interface, consisting of boxes relating to functions they control, making it easier to navigate the space.

U is for Unicode, a universal standard for encoding characters from all the world's languages, whatever the parameters.

It translates letters into characters we read everywhere we go, be it text files, web pages, and other types of documents galore.

V is for Viruses that infect your computer and are sometimes released by malicious users.

So, if you want to maintain your computer's health and preserve your files, pics and everything else, you will need to follow careful protocols to inoculate yourself.

VIRUS
VIRUS DETECTED

W is for Windows, not the kind you look out of.

But the computer operating system made
famous by Microsoft, when personal computers
were first offered to us.

X is for X86, a Central Processing Unit, the
brain of your computer providing speed and
performance.

X86 or the Pentium processor made famous
by Intel and not its competitor. The brain that
keeps the machine running smoothly and ever
faster into virtual reality.

Y is for YouTube, the home of videos. Spreading
music and knowledge and know-how like
never before.

Where you can become a superstar and influence
the lives of all.

Z is for Zip files, a little like zippers. In order to
access them, you will need a file ripper.

These files are compressed to stuff more info in
them. They take up less space on your hard drive
and are faster to transfer to other computers,
whatever the matter.

Altogether, A through Z, have taught me about
computer complexities, when I use my nice
device in my quest to reach the heights.